Designer Diaries

DESIGNER DIARIES

"The Mart Under the Rainbow"

By ROBERT DOBNICK

INDEX

Designer Diaries

ACKNOWLEDGMENTS

To Herb Schmidt my first love
Thank you for giving me direction

To Joe Gaul my mentor
Thank you for teaching me the ropes

To life partner Jack Hays
Thank you for loving me without reservation and making me the man I am
today

And to my husband Chadwick Godfrey
Thank you for saving me from myself and giving me new life in your love

INTRODUCTION

"A sadness seemed to envelope me as I stepped out into the crisp autumn air. Faces from long ago lurked in the shadows and the sounds of laughter echoed softy in my ears.

It had been forty some years now since I first knew this place. A life time of memories made in its halls and an eternity of emotions lay bare in its arms.

Time the universal task master had made my world over one more time and transformed yesterday into tomorrow again. But only time could tell where my new adventure might take me so I eagerly ventured forth into the new days light.

Who would have thought that one's life could be so controlled by a pile of bricks and stone? But then buildings are full of more than just interior spaces. They are energized by the people who inhabit them, and the ghosts of happenings that fill them with life.

For over forty years The Merchandise Mart was the center of my world, a place to work and play, a venue that hosted my professional life for several decades. It was both my mentor and my muse, but it was always a friend and confidant.

Entering its hallowed halls again, after a brief rest bit, was both invigorating and melancholy at the same time. The years had no doubt left their mark. The elegant upscale showrooms seemed a little less impressive, and the electric energy of years past was no longer there. But the memories still stay strong in my mind and will always be there as long as I am."

The Mart Under the Rainbow

In the Beginning ...

Once upon a time, in another universe, there existed as very special place in a very special metropolis called Chicago. The name of this special place was the Merchandise Mart!

The "Mart", as it has come to be called, is not just a building made from concrete and metal but rather the compilation of all the people and events that have happened there. It is a testimony to the supreme reality of decades of the creativity and decadence that did and still do drive my world!

The sensitive 60's had given way to the sexy 70's and life would never be the same again, for better or for worse. Interior Design as a profession had come into its own and with it a whole new culture. The beginnings of a society that would, at least for the moment, be more in tuned with art and creativity, with fashion and passion than ever before; A privileged group of social "wannabes" that would rock the very foundations of the design world.

Enter me, a hopeful from a small town in Illinois walking unabashedly into the mouth of the dragon. The city then was a strange mix, the art of the possible tempered with that of the not so much so, while exciting in its promise equally daunting in its restrictions. But for the hopeful it offered up at least a chance at a new and different life style. One thing that you realize early on in a small town or suburb is that different is not so much accepted unless you are rich or lucky. In Chicago you could create your own dream.

Imagine this, you have just left the closely monitored lap of conservative and somewhat rural America and landed in another country, so to speak. What do you do and where do you turn? For me it was easy. The first thing you do is everything that you didn't before. The new world is at hand and you are the explorer, so go for it right? Well not so fast, you see being raised by a Roman Catholic Mother, and more to the point Grandmother, there is that ever present guilt thing. However there is always a way around these dilemmas. My father was a martini man, at least early on, until the martinis turned into straight vodka from the bottle. But I digress, vodka has always been my drink of choice and so it was for the newly anointed movers and, shall we say, shakers of the era.

Chicago in the 60's and 70's was a land of wonder and opportunity. Not that it had changed any more than any other major city these last decades, but it was quite special then. OK, so there you have it. Small town boy comes to the big city and plunges into what will become his own very special world. Before the magical Merchandise Mart evolved into what would become the model for design centers nationwide. There was a small but elite enclave tucked away behind Saks Fifth Avenue, just off "The Avenue", by the name of The John Strauss Showroom. John Strauss, the owner and anointed prince of furniture, fashion and more, ruled the social scene from his posh and pretentious "to the trade only" showroom and thrown. John for one thing was the heir to the Fair furniture stores.

I had been lucky enough to be introduced to this world by my first partner, not necessarily a man of means, but rather more a mogul of the decadence of the time. I landed a job working for

Mr. Strauss' "part time" partner Dane Ackers, a noted Chicago Interior Designer by day and rollicking bon vivant by night. Dane was also fast friends with my partner Herby and thus there came an apprenticeship for me. For several years I was fortunate enough to experience la dolce vita at its best, parties that were legendary and affairs to remember.

Now while John Strauss was the Prince of the day, Richard Himmel was King. Mr. Himmel had carved out his niche as Design Diva in the Midwest. Mr. Himmel, originally an English teacher and novelist, had moved into the business of interior design with the help of his sister Muriel. Dick, as he was known to most, had now cast himself as the famous designer that would in fact become.

Muriel who had a bridal accessory shop on the north shore was instrumental in introducing him to the ladies who lunched. Dick wasted no time in getting to the top.

The Midwest in those days, interestingly enough, was becoming a power house in the new "business" of interior design and the Mart would become center stage. Designers who wanted to become a success had to, by rite of passage, pass through an internship at Mr. Himmel's temple of the arts and I did.

I remember working on the Clement Stone residence in Lake Forest (a very wealthy north shore suburb). The house was a beautiful old Adler mansion and had an entrance hall that rivaled that of Versailles. So many accoutrements were needed to fill the vast spaces that many a trip to Europe was involved. My friend Sheila (a self proclaimed witch) was Mr. Himmel's bookkeeper at the time; she & I would become fast friends.

One day Sheila came up to me holding a check. It was from the Stones. I gasped in amazement! It was in the largest amount that I had ever seen then, and one of the largest in my experience to date.

In the day I was fortunate to work with such super stars as Bruce Gregga, Bob George and Greg Stratman to name just a few. You see Mr. Himmel, while a huge success in his own right, was more of a showman than an actual designer. His background was that of an English professor and his fortune came, rumor has it, by way of Sister Muriel's bridal registry. His stable of talent was well known and respected on both the Gold Coast and the North Shore.

Well time for me to move on. Mr. Himmel had a unique way of refreshing his pool of talent. Once or twice a year he would separate the "wheat from the shaft" and bring in new and more promising apprentices while saying adieu to the less fortunate. This was for me however a stroke of good luck for it landed me with a woman designer by the name of Roz Mallin.

During this period "The Mart" did business as a secondary designer source. The showrooms for the most part were dealer lines mass produced in North Carolina who had moved from the other furniture Mart at 666 North Lake Shore Drive. There were a few companies whom were beginning a trend towards higher end design - Baker Furniture, Knapp & Tubbs, Interior Crafts to name a few.

While the 60's belonged to John Strauss, the 70's were owned by Roz Mallin. Roz was a self made success. Granted her husband, a senior partner at the law firm of Jenner & Block gave her substance, her tenacity as a formidable business woman was well known and respected in the industry. The years with Roz were good ones and my career began to blossom under her somewhat possessive vigilance. Eventually my desire to expand my world would take us to other venues. I had always thought that the design business was a bit unstable, especially if you don't come from money. Interestingly enough Roz was on the same page at that time and as we talked of other possibilities her industry connections started to connect. A man by the name of Doy Richter who owned a fabric company called Tressard in New York City had wanted to open a showroom at the newly found, possible Strauss competitor, the Merchandise Mart. For years the Mart had been a mish mash of lesser, more pedestrian showrooms none of which could approach the glamour of Strauss. But the time was right and with the help of our friends we planted the seeds of what would become an urban legend.

Not ready for prime time, Roz enlisted the help of her Sister Lavergne and a best friend Noreen. Both ladies had wealthy husbands and sons named Michael and Robert, thus the Michael Roberts Showroom, across the street from the Merchandise Mart, began. The name was a compilation of the son's of the owners, Roberts for Laverne and Noreen's first born and Michael for that of Roz. I do think that Roz might have thought of me as well but that is unsure. The success of the "Mart Annex" so to speak was such that the Mart itself approached us with the offer of showroom space in "The Building". To complete the coup d'état Roz and Doy began to assemble a collection of stellar players in the furniture and fabric empire. Not the least to head the cast was Robin Roberts's owner of the then legendary Clarence House Fabrics company and with the addition of Robin's ex-partner Jay Spectre, who created the design of the space, a new era, was born.

"Pink Floyd", as I called him was the go to contractor for Mart renovations those days. "Sometimes sober" Floyd was embedded in the Mart's tenant shuffle game like a cockroach in a well stocked pantry.

Showrooms would move or reconfigure rather often due the gain or loss of product lines. Every time construction was involved the Mart would make their percentage on the costs by charging a management fee. Hence, the Mart and old Floyd did pretty well in each and every transaction.

Floyd was not the best when it came to details. That was something every client needed to deal with, but his prices and connections made it worth the gamble.

One day, just after Floyd had finished hanging new fabric display wings in our expanded fabric and wallpaper section, a Lady by the name of Ethel Samuels was flipping through one of the new collections. Miss Samuels was one of the dowagers of design in those days, and a very important client. First I heard a groan and then a series of loud crashes. The fabric wings had pulled away from the drywall partitions and came tumbling to the floor in a cloud of dust. Apparently Floyd had underestimated the weight load of the new wings. Fortunately no one was injured and Ethel had escaped unscathed. She was however shaken to the core.

During the next decade I would be part of the wondrous world of the rich and infamous. An endless stream of celebrities would pass through the showroom doors and the parties seemed to never end, an opening, a new product introduction, or just any reason really to par-tay!

Let's now throw into the mix a few other elements. Phil Kelley, the new owner and president of the Knapp & Tubbs Showroom. Dick Himmel, who created a Chicago based power house of Deco and Decorator Nouveau decadence was known not only for their high end and "glitzy" product but for their infamous Market Parties.

Picture it, 1972 and a market party is underway. It is 5pm and the place is Interior Crafts. This is one of the legendary parties to which everyone who is anyone lusted for an invitation to. I was lucky enough to be one of the chosen Baker Furniture and merged the two into one colossal entity "Baker Knapp & Tubbs" which included manufacturers such as Henredon, Kindel, John Widdicomb and more. Jerry Seiff and Vito Ursini of Interior Crafts who with the help few thanks to the status of my employer at the time – Roz Mallin. People have often asked me if this was her real name and the answer is yes. The Roz was short for Roslyn and her husband Milton Mallin was a distinguished lawyer and senior partner in the firm of Jenner & Block in Chicago. Cocktails were being poured out to the masses and hors d'Oeuvres were being ground into the carpet and upholstery. The night after these orgies the factory workers would come in performs their miracles. By 9am the next morning the showroom would be cleaned, refinished and reupholstered and ready for another business day. At some point a tall very attractive "sample boy" from one of the other showrooms begins to take off his clothing on the dance floor and reveal his rather well endowed assets. This was to become a yearly ritual for a few years at least. In another corner of the showroom Mr. Himmel's "go for" Michael was becoming ill from way too many drinks and ended up face down, kissing the floor. While his limp body was being carried from the room it seemed as though he was levitating above the crowd like some sacrificial animal paying homage to the market gods, kind of a "Breakfast at Tiffany's" moment.

There were ever so many more moments of total abandonment and debauchery which seemed only to fuel the exuberance of this magical time.

Most nights just about the time we were ready to close up shop for the day, several of our loyal customers would pop in knowing that a cocktail hour could be had if only they asked. It was a lovely way to end a busy day, and a great way to begin an evening of more festivities.

Night after night the candle seemed to burn at both ends and as time pushed forward a few of the old guard would begrudgingly retire for the night.

There always seemed to be a party or event and the energy of the decade never seemed to be exhausted. It was like Studio 54 and Mardi Gras rolled into one.

Speaking of Mardi Gras, Dugan's Bistro was Chicago's answer to New York's Studio 54. Celebrities such as Rudolph Nureyev, Mick and Bianca Jaeger, Senator Edward Kennedy to name a few. The "Bearded Lady" would dance nightly and the crowd, which was mostly gay, would mingle comfortably with the hip straights making it the fashion spot for the glitter scene.

I remember an afternoon cocktail party at the Roz Mallin Showroom for Sheryl Wagner (a very posh line of bathroom faucets and hardware). One of our guests decided that she would like a remembrance of the event and removed a malachite encrusted door knob from a display and placed it in her purse. Roz had been watching her and at the appropriate time tapped her on the shoulder. "Will that be a charge or cash dear", Roz said very casually. The woman blushed and put the knob down. Exit stage left ...

As wild and raucous as the Interior Craft Parties were the Baker, Knapp & Tubbs parties were the essence of dignity and decorum. Perhaps the leader in high end mass marketing in those days Phil Kelley was an interesting mix of charm and elegance mingled with as masterful whit that could decimate adversaries from 20 paces. During the reign of King Phillip, Baker Knapp & Tubbs would become a leader in the furniture fashion industry. Collections would be introduced at High Point Market yearly from prominent furniture designers such as Alessandro, John Saladino, and Barbara Berry as well as collections such as Stately Homes of England and Historic Charleston.

When I was senior designer with Baker Knapp & Tubbs it was a golden age. Mr. Kelly had managed to sell the company to North American Phillips and to maintain his position as

President of the Baker. The money from this venture helped to finance the opening of BK&T showrooms around the United States as well as London, England. During the next 8 years I was privy to first class travels and many wonderful adventures. The Mart was indeed dropping its seeds around the country and the world too for that matter!

With the opening of a new Design Center there was always a spectacular event which consisted of cocktails and dinners with the elite of the day. Designers, actors, politicians and luminaries from all walks of life would clamor for an invitation to the festivities.

From San Francisco and Los Angeles to New York, Miami and all points between, the world passion was glamour in design and fashion.

San Francisco was a favorite of mine and quickly became a second home. With friends living across the bridge in Sausalito it became my second city for a while. But then so was Miami and Dallas. Oh wait! What about New York and Boston?

No doubt they were all my second cities, but Chicago would always be my touch stone and first love.

As all the major cities gave birth to their own Merchandise Marts I felt a special kinship as if I had helped in their development, perhaps because I had indeed.

Sex in the Cities

Along with the excitement of travel to these magical cities, there was also that after hours time that came along after the work day was completed.

When I started my travels with Baker I was newly divorced from my partner of 12 years. Dumped for a younger make and model as it were. So to compensate for my single status I decided to explore the benefits of long distance relationships. Once again, the Mart in her infinite wisdom had rescued me and given me a new beginning.

There was Izzy in New York and Puerto Rico, Woody in LA, Lane in Houston and Keith in Dallas. Each and every one of my new found friends brought with them a new and exciting element that filled my vagabond life with fun and friendship.

San Francisco was by far my favorite for fun and excitement. I had made a friend of a lovely couple who lived in Sausalito. Their house overlooked the city and bay.

Margret owned a porcelain importing company and supplied me with fabulous vases and other Asian accoutrements for my showroom displays. They had a guest bedroom on the first floor with its own entrance so I was free to come and go as I pleased. This made it all the more fun to visit since it didn't involve my padding an already rather hefty expense account, and I could extend my stays over a weekend when possible.

The mood in San Francisco those days was party city and my evenings out were to party plenty!

The Castro back in the 70's was the center of a divergent culture of free love and in the heart of the LGBT movement. There was seemingly something for everyone from leather to prep, and from all night disco to ballet and opera.

I spent many a night after work at a bar on Market Street, just east of the Castro, watching the magical San Francisco fog making its way down from Twin Peaks and eventually into the city on its way to the Bay.

Miami also held a special place in my heart. It was the first city that I ventured to in my new position as senior designer with the Baker collaborative. I basically lived there on and off for several months while restoring the showroom which had been devastated during the riots of 1980.

There was a fabulous Martini Bar in the posh Bal Harbor Shopping Center on Collins that served the best Rum Martinis, and the Puerto Rican bartender was very attractive too. Crush time!

Dallas and Houston were two other cities that became favorites. It was in Houston that my friend, Isabel Goettinger Spitzy, gave me my Texas Handle "Bobby Frank". I still wear it with pride whenever there.

Cowboys and Tea Dances where all part of the charm, and my days of Dynasty are still apart of many found memories.

Perhaps one of my most memorable moments during these years of jet travel and expense accounts happened at an event in New York , yet another showroom opening. An elderly but elegant lady by the name of Elizabeth Remsen was talking with my boss at the time Phil Kelly. As I walked by Mr. Kelly stopped me and introduced me to her. The amazing thing was that she remembered me, and I her, from years before when I had worked with her and Roz Mallin on her home in Remsenburg and her Park Avenue Mansion in New York. What a very small word it is indeed.

As the years wore on however, the constant travel and relentless partying took its toll. I had become jaded and estranged from my home and friends in Chicago and the Mart my Mentor was calling me home.

On a day warm day in July 1982, I met a man who would turn my world upside down. The Mart had once again given me a gift, and this gift would last for over 28 years!

Having a new partner in my life made the travel even more tedious and I wanted nothing more that to stay home and nest. It took a few years before I threw in the towel at Baker, but in the mean time Jack & I would have some fun and exciting adventures on the road!

I remember a time in San Francisco when, in order to enjoy a long weekend, Jack volunteered to help me accessorize the showroom so that we could leave early. It was a Saturday and the neighborhood was desolate. As we were working or magic we decided that it we needed more lamps. The lamps were kept in the emergency stair exit to the roof top. We both entered into the storage area forgetting that the door would lock behind us and it did.

The only way out was to go to the roof, and once on the roof there was no way down. No way except for an open window into the next door neighbor's space which we had found by following a cat who had happened upon us. Fortunately we were both a little thinner in those days and managed to enter the space.

Alarms immediately went off and we found ourselves running for the exit downstairs. Fortunately I did have the keys to the front door of our space thus managing to escape the police who had been summoned.

I believe that my new found partner was the main reason that I survived those eight years on the road. He gave me a purpose one again and a new and healthier direction in which to funnel my creative spirit, and to build a new life in which to grow and prosper. I had, for a time, abandoned my dreams and had started to listen to the reckless winds of decadence and indulgence.

Speaking of decadence, there was plenty of that when it came to design community in general.

Luminaries such as Jay Spectre, John Saladino and Dakota Jackson, to name a few, where ever present on the scene. Baker Furniture would employ a new talent every year to develop their new collections, and V.I.P.'s where a must on the list for every event.

At the opening of the Design Center in Washington D.C. I remember a rather famous designer, who shall remain nameless falling into me. I immediately noticed that she had obviously been over served and was in need of a little help. Having been in that position myself once or twice before, I can to her aide just as Carolyn Kennedy and her entourage where passing through. Time to exit stage left.

The Kennedy's, who owned the Merchandise Mart originally, had a presence at most events, Hollywood stars and starlets would make appearances and all would mix and mingle in the exuberance of Champagne and design that made for legendary soirees.

Of Revolution in Design and Morals

Part and party to this era of opulence was the sexual revolution that exploded around the same time. As if by decree from above the stars in heaven and on earth aligned and made for one hell of decade or two. Not to take away from the fact that this period in history was marred by a bloody war in Vietnam, political assassinations and cold war capers, but I believe that because of all the above and before mentioned events this era was begot.

I remember a hot night in August 1967 when a friend and classmate at art school introduced me to my first gay lover Herb and thus "the die was cast". That which had up until then remained illusion, all of a sudden become reality. Funny how such a little thing can become so important. But he was an attractive German guy with a most definite gregarious personality. He was a partner in a gay leather bar in Chicago and a pastry chef. We'll talk about the pastry chef later.

I was still in art school and he was my salvation father, lover and sponsor. As my first year of art school manifested itself I found myself totally liberated by the crazy but profound examples of my fellow artists, finding in them the ability to open my life to new and exciting adventures.

So seasoned by a year of art school, a dash of drugs and a new lover who taught me how to survive in the big city while cautiously watching over me, I began to bloom and with my new wings managed to fly higher than I ever dreamed. This was to be an age of enlightenment, a period of opulence and a decade to be dealt with; never before and perhaps never again would the mix be right to accomplish such a monumental endeavor.

The cast of characters was many and as varied as the arts would allow. Designers, writers, artists and such, all playing the same melody, a rich and rousing rhetoric that would establish Chicago and the country in general as the lead in furniture and fashion for decades. I can still hear the sounds of the Disco serenading the fashionistas as they danced and drank themselves into a creative frenzy.

Now, you may ask is this a healthy existence this decadence and debauchery that prevailed in this golden era, my answer would be yes! As my Grandmother told me once "remember you can do whatever you want in this life as long as you don't hurt yourself or anyone else". Compared to today's world of budgets, greed and downsizings my time seems naïve and rather festive in its innocence.

OK, here we go … What could be more exhilarating than to be present at the birth of an era?

Life as I have come to know it is merely a compilation of experiences that have occurred in ones existence but are indelibly registered in ones being. And so, my life experience was one of joy and liberation, one of innocence lost and of purpose given, a song of freedom but also a call to arms.

While the 60's was in some cases described as the counterculture and social revolution the era was also one of irresponsible excess and flamboyance in actuality the 60s have become synonymous with all the new, exciting, radical, and subversive events and trends of the period, which continued to develop in the 1970s, 1980s, 1990s and beyond.

Many monumental events started in the 60's – the Bay of Pigs, the Arab-Israeli conflict, the Cultural Revolution in China and the War in Vietnam nothing was quite as profound to me as the Stonewall riots which occurred in June 1969 in the New York City. The Stonewall riots were a series of spontaneous, violent demonstrations against a police raid that took place in the Stonewall Inn, in the Greenwich Village neighborhood of New York City.

They are frequently cited as the first instance in American history when people in the homosexual community fought back against a government-sponsored system that persecuted sexual minorities, and they have become the defining event that marked the start of the **gay rights movement** in the United States and around the world.

Believe it or not, this movement opened the road for me to explore my love for life and creativity. It was a magical time of healing for my anxious anxieties and a safe haven for a weary soul to nest. I am now strong.

I have always said that if you really want to know the soul of a culture just look at their role models. The 60's produces politicians such as John F Kennedy, Leonid Brezhnev and Mao Zedong; Musicians such as Bob Dylan and Joan Baez, John Lennon and Johnny Cash; and entertainers like Marlon Brando, Charlton Hesston and Julie Andrews will give you the idea of the tumultuous nature of the era. But in the background there always loomed that omnipresent Merchandise Mart which served as a backdrop to my play of life.

I must inject a foot note here since it was a very strong influence in my growth as a passionate and self assured gay man. My grandmother must be included in the roaster of "role models" for me. There was an event that occurred in 1970 that would reinforce my belief and commitment to my new life style and make it possible move on with my new found freedoms.

During a visit to my home town of Rockford, Illinois my new partner, at the time, he was introduced to my family in a ritual of vetting which can only be described as the circle of terror. This is the moment when the family gathers in a circle around the newly joined couple and determines whether or not the new member is worthy of acceptance into the family fold.

Grandma, ever the supreme matriarch, was always hovering between the kitchen and her throne. At just the right moment she would pop up, or out of, the kitchen and make a pronouncement bestowing her blessing or expressing her disdain. In this instance the direction of the conversation was most definitely aimed at the status of my partner and my relationship to each other. With the utterance of a single sentence this matriarchal sage would both establish her understanding and issue her acceptance of our life style.

Grandma had been my real mother growing up while my mother was more like an older sister. She instilled in me early on the two golden rules that would give me my direction and purpose in life.

First and foremost was this; be strong and true to yourself because you cannot help yourself or others if you are not healthy and strong.

Secondly, and equally important was; remember that you can and should do whatever you want to in life just as long as you don't hurt yourself or anyone else in the process.

Trust me, if for no other reason I am totally sure of one thing – had it not been for the sensitivity of the 60's coaxing me into a sense of security within myself I would not have made it to the 70's. This was a decade that will always define me and my generation.

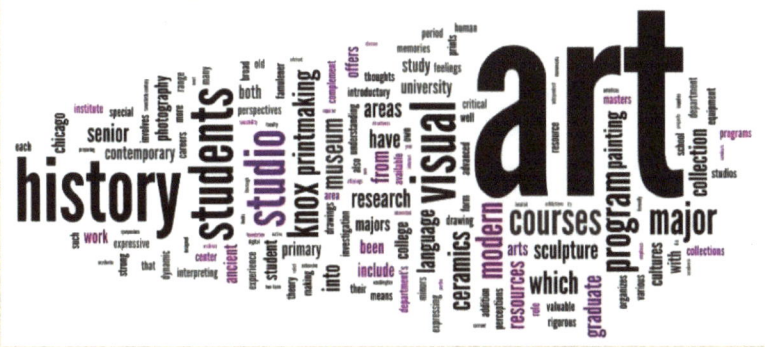

The Arts make a comeback!

While all of this is important, there is one thing that for me made the universe sing a different song – my flight from small town mid America to Metropolis Chicago. Without this defining transition I would not have become the vital person that I am today. Does art and design make a difference in society and culture? You bet, it totally is it.

The 70's and I were somewhat at odds with each other. I think that in retrospect so was the planet itself. While feminism and civil rights were coming into their stride art and architecture were seemingly stymied. My chance at becoming the next great fashion icon diminished as androgynous fashion and disco polyester became popular. Perhaps this was yet another resting place for the universe. After all how long can creativity persist without the intermittent intermission?

The 70's in my universe were a period of self searching; a time of reflection before progression; a moment in time for the beginning of a transformation. What happens when society in general takes a pause? Turn on the blender and let it rip! Hello disco and miniskirts, good bye classic sensibility and traditional tastes, maybe not so bad, but why does it take the extremes to bring us to balance, and why doesn't it last longer when we finally reach that moment of sanity?

My moment of sanity was reached when I found freedom in the arms of the enemy. My seemingly endless years of solidarity with partners and perseverance in business ended one summer's day with the realization that I was my own person. In that instant fashion, design and art itself changed for me as I watched the world grow cold and insensitive to life as I had come to know it, or maybe I had finally woken to it.

In the 70's all the passions of the 60's seemed to collapse into a giant ball of tasteless mass production. While the Mart and its followers made their way through this Dark Age, design itself suffered several crippling blows. What was once exciting and exhilarating became mundane but profitable. Enter me into Corporate American finding sanctuary in the very arms that were trying to strangle me.

In case you are not keeping track, we have now journeyed from the sublime to the ridiculous, the point at which galaxies collide and antimatter becomes the flavor of the day. It is times such as this that can make or break a culture. Many times in past centuries man has experienced such episodes. Decades or centuries when time seems to stop and take a long breathe before starting the next one. And so I did.

The Mart ever omnipresent and secure onto itself weathered many incarnations and has lived to remember them, as I have too. Once a child of hope and dreams I became a creature of survival and found that in that role I became stronger and more assured, if the Mart could survive this turmoil than so could I because it was in fact my sanctuary.

So from unabashed and elitist design, to the middle class metamorphic montage we finally, painfully arrive at the juncture of compromise. That place in time that really shouldn't exist. When compromise is the result of cost saving greed it has no place at the table.

Yet there we were in our new world of global coalitions and ever expanding downsizings leading us close and closer to the edge of oblivion; when cultures collide and morals collapse there begins to form what I like to refer to as a human black hole. Much like those found in outer space these human "black holes" manifest themselves when nature can't make sense of what is going on around it.

Open Those Pearly Gates

I had always stood in wonder of this place called the Merchandise Mart. The doors that one has to pass through in order to access its magic are much like "the Gates of Paradise"; you know the ones on the Baptistery of Saint John in Florence Italy. While the Baptistery Doors where designed by Andrea Pisano with the twenty top panels depicting scenes from the life of St. **John the Baptist** and the eight lower panels depict the **eight virtues** of hope, faith, charity, humility, fortitude, temperance, justice and prudence; the Doors to the Merchandise Mart where designed by Alfred Shaw showcase power and wealth of the Deco Era in Chicago and to pay tribute to a power broker of the day, Marshall Field. Entering through those doors I felt as if I was in a temple and I was.

Owned by Marshall Field and Company, the Merchandise Mart opened its doors to the public for the first time on May 5th,

1930. The structure realized Marshall Field's dream of having a single warehouse center for the entire nation and to do so, consolidated 13 different warehouses under one roof. Over the years the building has had several reincarnations. The Merchandise Mart was modernized in the late 1950s and 1960s. After years of being used by hundreds of government offices moving to the Pentagon, the purchase was followed by a renovation creating office space on the lower floors and promoting use of the upper floors for home furnishing and apparel showrooms. Even though other directions have been pursued by its owners, the building remains know mostly for its contribution to the Interior Design Industries and has been a model for many other design centers around the country.

More than all this however is the mystique that something exists in this structure that cannot be found elsewhere. There is a hallowed magic that exudes from its corridors and an aura of the awesome power in its design.

So what else can I say to instill in you the opulence of this edifice? Well maybe just that as all things exist for a purpose, this one existed and still exists because there is, and I hope always will be a need for a showcase of ultimate creativity and design at its best.

The Decades of Decadence

If the 60's where sensitive, the 70's where sexy, and the 80's, I don't know, maybe just decadent?

To achieve ultimate design freedom one needs to be free themselves. In order to create you must be uninhibited and free to be free. If there are constraints then they will or course restrain, and if there are limitations they will most certainly limit.

The procession of excesses in these years would give way to a new and perfected middle class that would in turn beget an era of never before seen common wealth. The idea of nirvana within the ranks of the masses would be realized, if only for the moment.

As for me I have always been lucky enough to find my own freedoms. Perhaps it comes from the fact that I have always subscribed to the belief in an ordered universe where joy is achieved by means of self knowledge and acceptance.

So then, in the 70's I discovered that there was more to design than just pretty colors, fun fabrics and expensive furniture. Design is really the order in the universe, it is the thing that makes us conscious of the marvels that surround us every day and defines our thoughts and feeling. Without it this would be a very bland and empty world.

It was in the 70's that my teachings from school took root and started to grow. My education had been the fertilization but my work experience would be the soil in which I would plant my roots.

I believe that it was most definitely The RozMallin Showroom that made the Merchandise Mart into the success it is today because before we opened the showroom the Mart was mainly a compilation of middle market furniture showrooms with no special style. RozMallin not only brought the high style, east coast designer lines from John Strauss to the building but introduced the newer and more contemporary designers from the west coast to Chicago as well.

I spent most of my waking hours at the Mart in the 70's and can remember many nights there as well. Back in those days there was a tendency to mix cocktails with business and with great success. Our showroom was known to have the best after hours bar in the building, especially because it was free. Everyday around 5pm our designers knew that they could relax at the end of tedious day of shopping with a cocktail at RozMallin. This of course would also encourage them to shop more at our showroom, and after a cocktail of two it was a lot easier to make decisions, right?

I know it seems like all we did in the 70's was to drink and party. Not true! We also worked very hard as well. Priorities were a little different back then and I'm not so sure that they weren't perhaps for the better.

The bejeweled Freddy Aldridge wearing his fur coats with his entourage; beautiful Bob George; and the serene Gregg Stratman all would grace our temple of design and drink at the altar.

I remember a day in June 1978. It was NEOCON and the design world was gathering in Chicago for spring market. All the luminaries were there from around the design world to put on a show, and what a show it was. Every showroom would try to get your attention by hosting events and offering refreshments. The economy was booming and everyone was making money hand over fist, except for me. This was also getting close to my swan song at Rozmallin before my new venture at Baker Furniture so I was feeling pressure from both sides, romantically and economically.

NEOCON

Neocon was an excuse every year to throw elaborate cocktail parties and party the night away to the sounds of disco music and all the accouterments associated with decadence of the era.

Much like Carnival in Rio or Mardi Gras in New Orleans, Neocon was a celebration of design and decadence coupled with the elite energy of international celebrity - a cirque du Soleil of the day. Many a misty memory still surfaces when the incantation is uttered!

Carpet companies would hold raucous cocktail hours while Contract Furniture companies would counter with tables of shrimp and caviar. The Residential Design showrooms would offer up a more sophisticated venue of designer cocktails and haute cuisine.

I remember a NEOCON in 1984 when the Design Atelier Showroom sponsored a "leather" party at a bar called the Ozone. The night was festive and both straight and gay designers drank and danced the night away, funny how a party with costumes and booze can loosen up even the most uptight individuals.

Social functions at the Mart were always driven by the social upper class and therefore of needs be posh and, if you will, over-the-top even. Therefore, panache was the mood and the Mart could and would always deliver. Even into the nineties she kept step and, while maybe not quite as gilded as the previous decades, her many facelifts and tucks have kept her as desirable as ever.

The Contract Showrooms, catering to the booming corporations would throw fantastic parties, inviting swarms of designers and architects to open bars and endless seafood buffets.

The lesser residential showrooms would compete for attention on a more intimate level, but certainly no less lavish, and definitely more chic.

If I remember correctly there was one showroom that actually brought an elephant to their space – I'm not sure why, but it did raise eyebrows. Other showrooms would import celebrities and even trendy sports cars to their venues in order to outdo. If Cirque du Soleil had been around they most certainly would have been on the list!

There was always a sense of devil-may-care in those days, an electric atmosphere that kept things light and even though good times were had, business went on as usual. As I look around me today I don't understand how the landscape of doing business has become so morose. The enjoyment seems to have been sucked out and the joy left as a dry bitter shell that is unpalatable.

The days, or rather nights of Dugan's Bistro had faded and with it the driving disco music with its golden group of Divas had fallen silent. It was, if you will, "the day the music died".

All in all these were golden years in the furniture industry before the "made in China" mentality tore at the fabric of its soul and rendered it impotent.

Today the new generations like the Eco Boomers, Millennials and Gen Z Kids stroll through the sterile hallways dressed in their kinky but conservative clothing and sip their sodas and such. I do see a trend towards the sensibilities of the 50's beginning to manifest in the Gen Z Kids especially so maybe all is not lost in the dull conservatism of the last ten years.

Maybe the Mart has finally wakened from its long winter's nap and will weave its spell once more for old time sake.

As I mentioned earlier, the 70's to me meant RozMallin but they were also round two of my love affair with my second partner Joe Gaul. I had brought Joe into the fold at RozMallin when we were still in the Revlon building across the street, the showroom then still known as Michael Roberts. Joe had helped take the showroom in the right direction and played a critical part in its success. So to me 1978 was not just another NEOCON, rather it was a major turn for me in all directions. But with change comes opportunity and so I seized it and began yet another adventure.

During the last two years of the 70's I found myself traveling the country working as a senior designer with Baker Furniture and becoming a stronger and more independent person because of it. I would travel from Chicago to LA, to San Francisco. Live in Miami for a few months rebuilding a showroom, and play cowboy "Bobby Frank" in Houston & Dallas, Texas with my new found Baker family.

The Mart however was always there with me in those times too since my home office was still Chicago and I would return for a recharge every now and then. In fact, the Mart is and has been my recharging station for over 40 years now. I can hardly remember a time or occasion when the Mart was not involved in one way or another. In a way it has always been my lover and protector.

On the Road Again

During my stint at Baker Knapp &Tubs my horizons most definitely widened not only through travel and experience but also with the knowledge of self that comes when the responsibility of maintaining order is coupled with the sometimes lonely world of "transient" meditation, if you will ...

From San Francisco to Miami and LA to New York, my life began to fill with the opulence that exists in the power capitals of North America. Looking back now I believe that it was these exposures that filled me with the hunger to travel further into the wondrous world of international design.

If nothing else, Roz Mallin had taught me one very important lesson, and that was that the world of high fashion and design knows no boundaries; whether geological or cultural, good design is everywhere and in everything. What, I thought, would happen if I could design my life by using the same principles: unity, harmony and balance?

Over time I would find that these same principles would save me from the dangers of excess as well as give me the courage to pursue my passions with discretion and the sophistication that comes from self assurance.

Whether at home in Chicago or traveling through Europe and South American my "Mart" mentality served me well and gave the confidence to enjoy the world of total design!

To this vary day I find myself filled with a passion for design and, being an Aquarian by nature, finding design in my travels.

The Designers

Interior Design became a profession around the turn of the century. In America, <u>Candace Wheeler</u> was one of the first woman <u>interior designers</u> and helped encourage a new style of American design. She was instrumental in the development of art courses for women in a number of major American cities and was considered a national authority on home design. However, it was Elsie De Wolfe that who refined it.

Interior design was previously seen as playing a secondary role to architecture. It was not until later that specific representation for the interior design profession was developed. The US National Society of Interior Designers was established in 1957, while in the UK the Interior Decorators and Designers Association was established in 1966. Across Europe, other organizations such as The Finnish Association of Interior Architects (1949) were being established and in 1994 the International Interior Design Association was founded.

Ellen Mazur Thomson, author of *Origins of Graphic Design in America* (1997), determined that professional status is achieved through education, self-imposed standards and professional gate-keeping organizations. Having achieved this, interior design became an accepted profession.

Much as a play has its characters so did the Mart, each and every one performing their own unique and individual part.

I believe that Interior Design actually became a legitimate profession in the 60's and 70's.

Chicago already had its cast of characters and the Merchandise Mart would be their theatre.

While Dick Himmel was the king, he begot many of Chicago's most successful designers. People like Bruce Gregga, Richar, Gregg Stratman and Robert George to name a few.

Robert George was one of my favorite people. A handsome and genuinely good man, Bob worked for Mr. Himmel at the time I made his acquaintance. Soon after Bob George would become Robert George and a sought after and talented designer in his own right.

Bob had a style all his own in both interior design and men's fashion. You could see him at the Mart with clients in tow, sometimes wearing his Abercrombie & Fitch monkey hair coat or one of his many flashy capes. As he would sweep through the corridors of this cathedral of design, it was as if the curtain had just gone up for act 1 of a new play. Being a successful designer then meant that you must be unique, a character if you will, and he was that and more.

One day while we (RozMallin) were still located at the "Mart Annex" Bob came in the showroom to shop. It was during spring market and he was fresh back from some exotic location. Tanned and buff, he was wearing a light beige linen jump suite; it was sleeveless and had a V neck that plunged to his navel. Shirley, our receptionist then, was seated at the front desk and as he bent over to sign in it was apparent that he was commando as well. I believe that Shirley smiled for a week after that encounter.

Not to be out done, Greg Stratman, a much more reserved person, used his boyish good looks and quiet demeanor to attract attention. Although I did see him on occasion gracing a market party in a silver lame jump suit or sheer shirt and slacks.

Both Greg and Bob were true gentlemen and beautiful peacocks as well.

Enter Robert Mellon, an older but still handsome man. Bob dressed the part of an aging ingénue. Stoic and I'll tempered as he was there was another side to him that was rather endearing.

One thing that I learned from Bob was that if you wanted something out of life you had to grab the reins and own the moment. Life is not for the faint of heart and success is a fickle friend at best.

My first apprenticeship was with a man by the name of Dane Akers. Dane was rash and electric personality. His partner at the time was the owner of the elite showroom just off the Avenue, and I met him through my partner at the time.

During that time I also made the acquaintance of a rather austere young man by the name of Dale Hollingsworth. Dale was Dane's right hand man back then. While standoffish in the beginning we would eventually become best friends meeting several years later at a showroom opening for Baker Knapp and Tubbs in San Francisco.

While working for Dane I met a young woman from Texas who became part of our team. She basically ran her design business through Dane's firm. It was only a matter of time before she became very successful.

One day she showed up one driving a Mercedes Benz, a present from an enamored client. A week or two later she appeared in a full length mink coat. Finally a rather large diamond was seen on her finger. I couldn't help but wonder if maybe she was providing more than just design assistance.

Following my time with Dane, I served time with a man by the name of John Ksander. John was an angry man. He would start the day with can of Tab and a temper tantrum.

John had figured out his recipe for success. Mr. Ksander had three basic floor plans and three color schemes. Every client would get one of the combinations and everyone seemed to be happy with the formula.

John and I seemed to have personality conflicts quite often. It seemed that there was no way to please him, but I vowed that I would hang in there for at least one year so as to have the experience documented on my resume.

My position lasted almost exactly one year. We parted ways after an intense argument over a fabric that was incorrectly ordered. To this day I believe that is was John's fault, but then he was the boss, so off I went to start another adventure.

As time fled by the cast and characters changed from year to year and decade to decade. Once the freshman I seem now to have become the teacher and sage.

There are times in life when you find yourself lost in the energy that is life, but time, you will find is in fact the master after all and to listen to it and let it in is the ultimate answer.

There is also a time in every one's life I think that sets its tone. What tone you may ask? It is the tone that defines your "life path" and for that matter your very existence.

I have been extremely lucky in my life to have had so many positive associations and involvements, so many people that have touched my life so deeply and sincerely. I believe that when one finally connects to life you feel the energy of a million or more Galaxies colliding in unison and giving birth, if you will, to your own reality.

Sometime, a long time ago, I found myself afloat on a sea of introspection, a place of indecision and a time of confusion. What was it that sparked that turn around, that decision to decide, that entrance into my "me"? Maybe it was the happiness of a summer's day spent with a fond friend, a night spent with a special lover, or maybe just the fact that I had in fact so many options in my life I thought that they would never run out. If only I could just make one of them real. Enter then reality, the moment of meaning, the ultimate end to the quest, my connection to my "other half".

Now it would seem that from the ultimate would come total satisfaction but not so. We are after all creatures of creation and thus are compelled to a life of endless evolution that is until we can no longer evolve or do not desire to do so.

Eventually I feel there is a gateway, a pass or a window that opens in the end to yet another tomorrow of unending beginnings, and those beginnings become an end unto themselves. So, on we go forever forward ever searching for another moment of meaning.

The Eighties

Bring on the 80's; A decade of personal growth for me with a new Company and a time of emotional growth in finding my inner self at last or again.

During this period the RozMallin Empire was beginning to collapse and a new comer was rivaling its position of power. A lady by the name of Holly Hunt would buy the RJ Randolph Showroom from John Strauss' widow Barbara and begin her ascension as queen of the Mart.

The 80's brought with it many things. It empowered and embraced the decadent life style of the time as well as defines it. I must admit however that I was not all that comfortable with this period; I found it to be a little too self-indulgent. Still the rebel of the 60's this sort of behavior didn't compute. Knowing what I do now however I would gladly return for an encore. It was a time of drama and decadence but at time of rebirth and restoration as well.

The decade did empower me to be freer and thus more successful. The best part about the 80's for me however occurred at, where else, the Merchandise Mart of course. It was there that I met my life partner and the love of my life, Jack Hays. Jack was a warm and gracious man with a boundless energy which could be felt from across the street. Jack and I would make our way through life for the next decades sharing our passion for design, for each other, and begin our own interior design business, but I digress. It was not over just yet.

Everyone has a place, a talisman, a touch stone if you will. Mine seems to be the Merchandise Mart. Much like Alice through the looking glass our life became as large or as small as we could imagine.

More Tales of The Mart ...

The tales of the infamous Merchandise Mart are many and more. Each and every designer and architect has I'm sure their own special experiences, and each of us has been touched forever by them.

To say that my world was forged in this edifice of metal and stone would be an understatement, the romance of the corridors of marble and silk where a beautiful backdrop for a most special and elaborate life, and working with the rich and famous was an interesting experience as well as a most important lesson.

Working with the tools of my trade I was enabled to create great beauty and lend a hand to those in need of transformation. Whether it was designing a mansion or making something special out of a workman's cottage, the same principles of time and space would apply.

There was a project in New York when we moved a couple from their elegant Lake Shore Drive apartment to a new penthouse in New York overlooking Central Park. While money was not a concern space most definitely was.

The main issue was a small window in a closet in the Master Suite. The client needed more space for her wardrobe but did not want to sacrifice the view, however small it was.

We finally had to make a decision, window or no window. I remember very vividly to this day my client lying down on the floor and crying in front of all.

The decision was finally made, but it did make for a rather embarrassing moment.

Another project that remains embedded in my mind was the day that we installed a two story spiral staircase in a penthouse residence on East Lake Shore Drive in Chicago. Because of its size and girth it was necessary to bring it up by helicopter.

What a spectacle it was to see and the fact that the streets around us had to be closed to traffic during the install made it even more glamorous.

It was not only the wealthy clients who could present challenges; many an upwardly mobile mogul could create drama as well. Even when money is no object frugalness can occur.

On a warm day in May, I met a new client at their newly purchased apartment across from Grant Park in Chicago. As we were discussing the scope of work, which was considerable, I was informed that we had a rather tight budget. The couple was moving from overseas to a new life in Chicago and needed to watch their pennies for now. This of course had no bearing on the fact that they still wanted only the best.

I am still amazed at how I was able to pull that one off, but by pulling some strings and uttering a few incantations our goal was achieved and I was heralded as a hero.

Many a residential project would punctuate my portfolio, but equally important was my roller coaster ride with corporate America. During the 80's, our country was bustling with the energy of a thousand engines of newly discovered commerce. The word "monopoly" would seem to have been removed from the collective vocabulary, Big Pharma in the guise of Monsanto, G. D. Searle, and NutraSweet to name a few.

My involvement with Monsanto started with a small offshoot of G. D. Searle called NutraSweet. Eventually G. D. Searle would be bought by Monsanto and NutraSweet would be sold to a private investment company, these entities would keep us busy for over a decade and thrust us into the lucrative lap of Corporate America.

Once ensconced as consultants to the billion dollar businesses of the day, our reputation would soon bring us to play with several other related industry giants.

Our corporate involvements would begin to wane in the down sidings of the 90's, and the bottom would all be drop out in 2001 with the World Trade Center tragedy.

As our focused turned back to residential projects, a new area enveloped us and, once again we would be reinvented.

I think that perhaps it was the fact that I had such a vast and diverse apprenticeship, with so many talented and demanding teachers that gave me the knowledge and discipline to accomplish and forge ahead in my chosen trade.

Fortunately I have also been blessed with friends and family over the years who have given me the support and encouragement to achieve my goals.

Design in the Millennium ...

As the world settled into the Millennium I was faced with yet another dilemma. Our Corporate "cash cow" had begun to disappear, as the ever tightening budgets became the new order of business.

Share holders were demanding bigger profits and the global outsourcing was forcing companies everywhere to tighten their belts.

This of course would mean a restructuring of our design business as well. Fortunately our business structure had always been flexible and we could grow our shrink as needed through the use of consultants and part time help.

When money was tight we would pull back and relax, thanks in part to our diligence and frugalness during the "glory days".

As all this happening, we were also getting a little older and the necessity to deal with our aging bones would make it even more of a challenge.

Enter the advent of global discontent, wars raging in the Afghanistan and Iraq, it was strange and surreal time for the nation.

What to do when faced with uncertainty and despair? Why throw a party!

In the design business, especially the residential design business, things are never constant or secure. One year could be stellar and the next not so much.

As clients come and go hopefully you reach a point at which the rotation becomes more controlled. However, when faced with all the trials and tribulations occurring during this period, there are no assurances.

Once a year we would throw a "Spring Fling"! Not only to remind our friends both old and new, that we were still standing, but also as a thank you for their past business and continued friendship.

The showrooms of the Merchandise Mart were trying to reinvent themselves too. With the discount mentality rampant and the new internet discounters chipping away at profits , nothing was the norm anymore, and free style entrepreneurships became the new standard.

And Now What ...

On September 11th 2001 the world would be changed profoundly by a handful of terrorists who would give their lives to avenge a misguided attempt at the destruction of a corrupt capitalist system that had become greedy and insensitive to the poor and middle class of the world, by killing thousands of innocent men, women and children. This would bring on a 10 plus year war which would only prolong an inevitable and disastrous killing field that threatened the very existence of life as we knew it. The Merchandise Mart and capitalism survived but were changed. The following financial crisis would rock the very souls the human kind but in the end we again would survive. So many global disasters would come and go but the Mart and I survived and prospered.

On November 14th 2009 however an event would occur that turned my world upside down and threatened to destroy my being and crush my soul. My beloved partner and long time companion of 28 years was taken from me by a sudden and unexpected heart attack. This time I was mortally wounded and even the Mart with all its power and glory could not comfort me. This time was different because it wasn't about possessions or money. It was about pure and unadulterated love and life itself.

For almost two years I wondered the country trying to run from the truth but inevitably the truth would always catch up to me. My life seemed empty and useless - loneliness was my constant companion and silence surrounded me.

Until one day I forced myself out of my office and back to the Mart, the place that had given birth to me and my career - the place at which half of my life had been lived. Taking small steps at first I began the process of healing and regeneration, reinventing myself one more time.

As I breathed in the air that was so familiar, infused with aromas of textiles and waxed wood, I began to feel at home. Even though many of the inhabitants were no longer there the building itself was and stood every bit as strong and proud as ever - as if to say "I am here for you and always will be ... welcome home"!

A few months later as I was talking through the halls of the Merchandise Mart I noticed an attractive young man who apparently had noticed me as well! A warm feeling came over me. It was as if the Mart in its benign wisdom had again given me a reason to go on and a way to find happiness one more time. The magic was still there under its rainbow. Although burnt and burnished in the aftermath of the ecstasy my Phoenix would rise again.

Chadwick Godfrey and I married on February 6th, one day after my 66th birthday, in Palm Springs California and are living happily back in Chicago. We still frequent the hallowed halls of the Merchandise Mart and, I'm sure will do so for years to come.

My child of the sixties who became an apprentice of life in the eighties, went on to become a man of knowledge with a passion for design and beauty in the nineties. But the dawning of the Millennium would temper my soul and forge a new person, with all the qualities of the past but made stronger by the promise of an even brighter future.

Life really is magical!

From Ashes to Air ...

There comes a time in one's life when a moment defines you. I have had several of those moments and each one has been unique and special, each adding to my living mosaic and sealing its sensitivities in their wake.

Even though the Merchandise Mart is no longer the force it had been in the past decades neither are most of the institutions from those earlier times. The lesson learned, if there in deed is one, is that life exists as a continuum. It neither starts nor stops for anyone. Life is in and of itself and we are merely attachments in time.

It has been almost eight years ago now that my life stopped abruptly and a long period of hibernation occurred, kind of a nuclear winter if you will. But during that long winters nap I was privy to another incarnation. That which had ended became fulfilled and all the feelings of the decades that had passed before became one for me. I had become strong. I had become my own man. And I had healed.

There was a new generation out there surging and filling the rivers and valleys of life. A new sensibility was being created and I was faced with the choice of jumping in again or staying behind on the mountain top. I must say there is a lot to be said for standing alone, but one cannot survive forever there. Stagnation leads to annihilation and I was certainly not ready for that.

I had been mentoring friends and colleges for many years without really knowing it. It was a good feeling to be able to help another with their life and career. Some of my worst battles have been fought within me, but I always found that the answer was therein as well. So maybe the answer to life's riddle of sustainment is self containment, but that containment must be shared.

In the years since my deluge I have become comfortable with myself again and have even began a new life partnership with a lovely younger man. Chadwick came into my life at just the right time. Just when I thought that mountain top was going to become permanent, he lifted me up and we sailed away together.

Living life again through his eyes is a beautiful and awesome thing. To be able to feel things long since gone as new is breathtaking.

We celebrated our first year anniversary together in Paris, city of lights. And we have since purchased a new home together. My business has become refreshed again and I feel like I am younger for it.

So what of the Mart and its place in this new age? It, much as I, have survived and actually prospered. Both of us are still functioning and mentoring a new crop of designers and artisans. Reliving and retelling stories of past glories has become part of my persona and I do enjoy occasionally pontificating on certain topics, after all what is life all about if not the remembering?

Oh, and yes I am still writing and creating new stories as well, after all someone has to do it, and this is just the beginning ...

The Denouement ...

"And as the tide of emotions began to recede, he saw a new and virgin shore, nourished by the very tides that had almost drowned him, a new shore to cast his seeds upon and a new place to call home. Could this be the dawning of a new age for Aquarius?

With hope and faith in his pocket and a light stride in his strep, the aging Aquarius found a new and gentle place to work and play, and to make right the day.

So many times when life throws us a curve we are immediately thrown off balance. But in the end the important thing to remember is that it is only temporary and only as disorienting as we let it be. There is much truth to the saying that we reap what we sow, but it is also true that we must constantly do damage control in order to keep our fields fertile and disease free.

I have noticed recently that there is a plethora of discontent in the world, almost as though there are no happy places left in which to take refuge. The secret however is just the opposite - there are in fact as many and perhaps more safe havens in this sometimes, made melancholy menagerie than we may think.

Today I am headed out into the storm again but this time I am prepared. So let life do its worst, I shall in turn do my best and leave the rest to fate ..."

BIOGRAPHY OF THE AUTHOR

Robert Dobnick was born in the heartland of the great Midwest, in Rockford, Illinois in 1948. At the time it was known as the Forest City because of its canopied boulevards of Dutch elm trees leading to lush parks and green spaces. Being part of the early baby boomers after World War II, I was fortunate enough to be raised in an era of unrivaled economic expansion by parents who were second generation citizens and middle class workers.

My mother's side of the family were farmers and artisans with grandmother being cook, baker and pianist, and grandfather a wood carver and farmer, my father's side where emigrants fleeing the genocide that occurred after the war in Belarus.

My passions have always been focused on the arts, and while pursuing a degree in both art and mathematics, I eventually gave over to the arts. Studying at the Chicago Academy of Fine Arts I realized that Interior Design would be the best way to accomplish what I desired most. The ability to direct artisans and trades as a symphonic unit was exciting, with the end result bringing a successful living environment and a happy and grateful client as well.

Graduating from design school in 1970 with a bachelor's degree in interior design I secured a position with a high end residential interior designer and began my career in residential design. During the many years to follow I found myself working for small and large design firms in many and varied capacities until I established my own practice in 1980. It was during the 80's that I first started mentoring younger designers and teaching evening courses for Latin School parents at Marshall Field's in Chicago.

My career has been most colorful and prosperous, but now I am finding that writing and teaching are the direction that I prefer to proceed in. After publishing three books, one on bereavement and the other two on rehabilitation and rebirth, I am most excited about passing on my expertise and experiences on to a new generation of creative individuals.

BIBLIOGRAPHY

I would like to thank all the people who have given me inspiration over the last years and helped me to understand life through their actions, their careers, and their mentoring. You know who you are.

And a special thanks to the Merchandise Mart for nurturing me throughout my career in the wonderful world that is design.

www.ingramcontent.com/pod-product-compliance
Lightning Source LLC
Chambersburg PA
CBHW041500280526
45792CB00004B/1079